Sails, Paddles and Rail

How the outside world came to Spurn Point in times gone by

Phil Mathison

Published by Dead Good Publications
Newport
East Yorkshire
HU15 2RF

©2020

All rights reserved. No part of this publication may be reproduced, stored in a retrieval system, or transmitted, in any form or by any means, without the prior permission of the publishers.

Other titles by the author

The Dead Good DADGAD Book
(ISBN 9780954693701)

The Dead Good Wacky Chord Book
(ISBN 9780954693725)

Shed Bashing with The Beatles
(ISBN 9780954693732)

The Spurn Gravel Trade
(ISBN 9780954693763)

Edited by: Captain Arthur Mathison - Now the long trick's over
(ISBN 9780954693770)

The Saint of Spurn Point
(ISBN 9780956299406)

Tolkien in East Yorkshire 1917 - 1918
(ISBN 9780956299413)

On Macabre Lines
(ISBN 9780956299420)

The Legendary Lost Town of Ravenser
(ISBN 9780956299437)

All Washed Up
(ISBN 9780956299444)

ISBN 978-0-9562994-5-1

Published by Dead Good Publications
Newport
East Yorkshire
HU15 2RF
©2020

Contents

Foreword — Page 5

Visitors — Page 7

Sailing Boats — Page 45

Paddle Steamers — Page 53

Motor Craft — Page 69

The Railway and Sail Power — Page 73

Appendix: Recreating a Spurn Legend — Page 85

Bibliography — Page 99

Front Cover

Image from 'Jackson's Guide to Grimsby Docks, Cleethorpes, & Neighbourhood' showing Victorian ladies in bustles enjoying a walk with their partners near Smeaton's Lighthouse on Spurn c1880.

Rear Cover

Great Central Railway poster advertising a trip from New Holland to Spurn in 1911, and a humorous picture postcard c1900 by the artist 'Cynicus'.

Foreword

During the twenty five years that I have researched Spurn Point, I have perceived that, especially prior to World War 1, much of its social and commercial history was allied with the Lincolnshire side of the Humber Estuary. Indeed, until the military road was built down the peninsula during WW2, the journey by road through Holderness was decidedly difficult, and visitors from this quarter less numerous than the great many waterborne excursionists who arrived by rowing boats, sailing vessels, paddle steamers and ultimately by motor cruiser. This profusely illustrated book is an examination of the people who visited this fascinating place from the early 19th century onwards.

I would like to acknowledge several people who have provided assistance with this book. First must be my wife, Mary, an excellent proof reader. Jan Crowther as always has been generous with her assistance and with permission to use several images. Next is Andy Gibson, who has spent many years working for the Yorkshire Wildlife Trust, first at the Spurn Nature Reserve, and latterly, covering much of the Humber area generally. The Hull History Centre has likewise proved invaluable at many points in my research. Mention must be made of Jennie Cartwright (nee Mooney) at Grimsby Library, who has always risen to the challenge of supplying me with the photocopies and any information on Spurn that she discovers. I am deeply indebted to Liz Betts of Barton upon Humber, who provided me with a CD of images of her relatives on Spurn around 1900. Finally, I would like to mention Matthew Jones and his grandfather John Dennis Major (who grew up on Spurn in the 1920s) for some of the background information, and also Roland Stork of Bridlington for the image on page 72.

If I have missed anyone else out, trust me, any help with my research, no matter how small, has been appreciated, and I hope that the end result presented here is some small recompense for any input I have received from many people over the years.

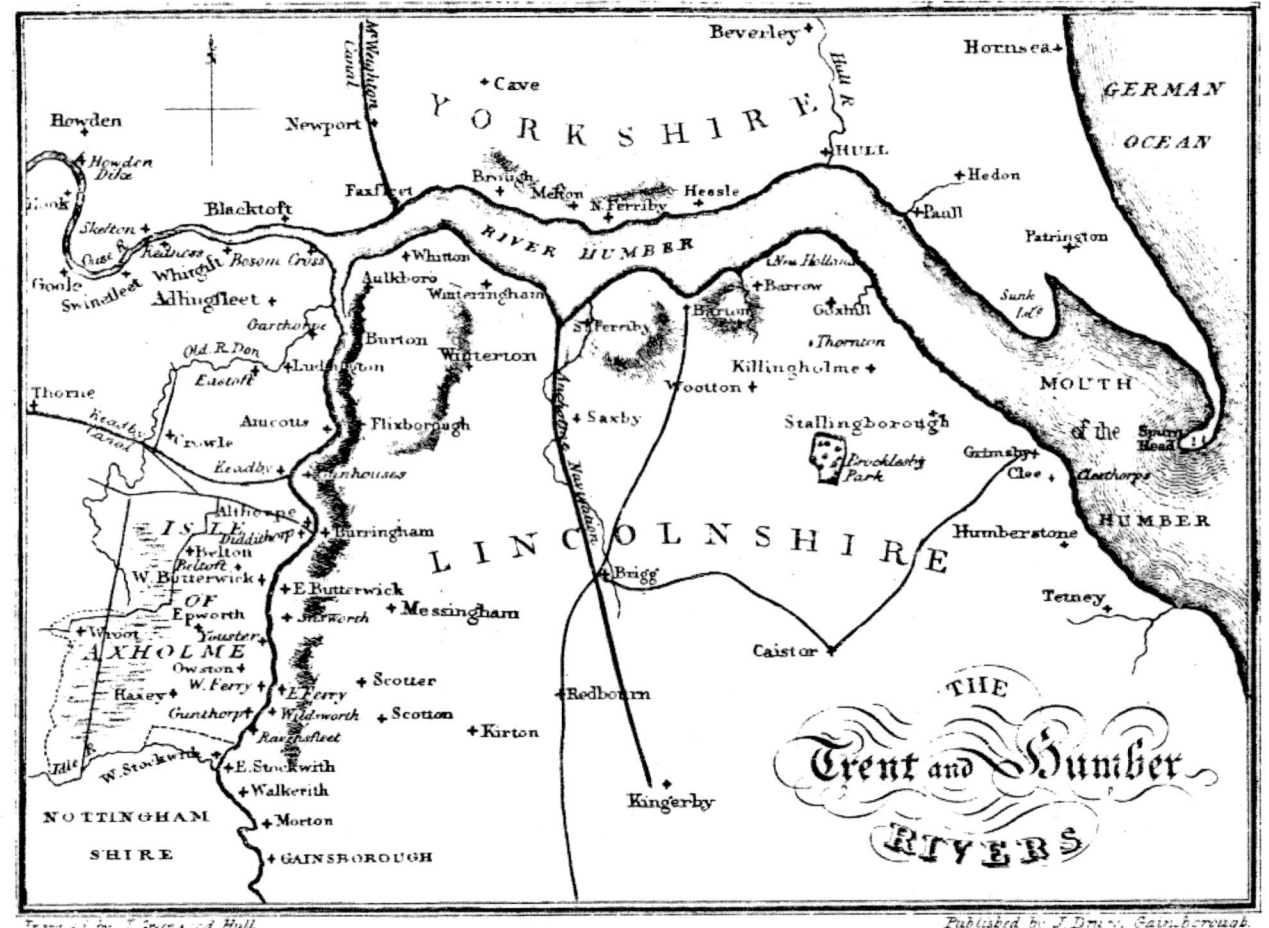

Map from 'The Trent & Humber Picturesque Steam Companion - J Greenwood, Hull 1833

The Visitors

Nowadays, anyone planning a day out at Spurn Point would travel through gentle Holderness countryside and arrive at this fascinating place via Easington. Turn the clock back a century and day trippers, (and there were many of them if the surviving postcards are to be believed), arrived not from Yorkshire, but mostly from across the water – Grimsby and Cleethorpes. There was a steady trade in conveying holiday makers across the River Humber on schooners and paddle steamers. The famous Spurn military railway from Kilnsea was not built until 1915, and was never intended for tourists, although it was used unofficially on occasion! Local firm Connor & Graham were providing a bus service to Easington by 1921, but a road down the point lay even further in the future, not being built until 1941. The delights of the peninsula for day trippers travelling by motor car would have to wait until after WW2. Looking at the records of early travellers to the peninsula, we can get an idea of the difficulty of accessing the Point via land. George Head, on a visit to Spurn overland in 1835 recorded 'The narrow ridge was a hard journey on foot or on horseback. Any wheeled vehicle found it awkward in the extreme. The narrow neck was covered by sands and marram grass (the bents), and by the sea when there were exceptionally high tides. Most carriages found it impossible, and usually travelled part of the way on the Humber clays.' It is little wonder that few came by land until the later 19th century. (Jan Crowther – The People along the Sand P24) On page 34, a visit by Walter White in 1858, also overland, notes 'As it is, the walking is laborious: you sink ankle deep and slide back at every step, unless you accept the alternative of walking within the wash of the advancing wave.' He discovered materials left over from work on the 1849 breach - 'The trucks, rails and sleepers with which the work had been accomplished were still lying on the sand awaiting removal.' Apparently then, the military railway of 1915 was not the first iron road laid on Spurn!

Roy Benfell, in his title 'Spurn Lifeboat Station – The First Hundred Years', page 35, contains the following information on the excursionists who arrived via the river, and their reception on the Point. 'The women tried to earn a little money by catering for visitors. Besides the gravel and fishing boats, paddle steamers brought day trippers from Hull and Grimsby, there were works outings, Sunday School celebrations, church groups and many others.' The scale of the number of excursionists can be judged by a visit on Thursday 20th May 1852 when a tea party of 1600 landed! (P75) On July 10th 1865 a party of three hundred visitors were expected, employees of Messrs Foster and Andrews works on an outing by paddle steamer from New Holland.

A tragic incident occurred on July 8th, when 'A small group set sail for Grimsby to buy supplies to cater for the party. The good, clear weather gave way to a sudden summer storm and John Marshall, a lifeboat man, dropped dead in the boat. At first it was thought he had been struck by lightning, but it was later decided he had died of fright.' (P101) Later visits noted in Benfell's book are, on page 122, 'The Duke of Edinburgh visited Spurn and was taken fishing by Winson 15th August 1881, and a further royal visit is recorded when Prince Louis of Battenburg and party visited on 30th June 1893. (P136) The Archbishop of York had conducted a service at Spurn earlier in the same month.

I have only discovered one work of fiction that alludes to these intrepid early travellers to Spurn. Again these visitors came from across the Humber. An author with the enigmatic name, E.L.F., wrote a book entitled 'Our Home in the Marsh Land' (published by Griffith Farran Browne & Co of London in 1877). On page 40, the main character notes:

'Spurn Point is unlike anything I have ever seen anywhere else, and I scarcely know how to make my description clear to those of you who have only seen the common sorts of country. Imagine a long, narrow promontory running out for miles into the sea, and consisting solely of low, wave-like hills of loose white sand. Most of these are covered with a peculiar kind of grass, so thinly that you can easily count the separate blades in a square foot. It is long and wiry, - I rather think that the Spanish esparto, used for making paper, must resemble it when green. This odd-looking grass, with a few tiny curious plants, is the only vegetation of any sort on the Point. It is so low that one part, near the mainland, is entirely covered by high tides, and the Point becomes an island.

We landed very near the smaller lighthouse, for there are two, - one built almost in the sea, and reached at high tide by a wooden bridge; the other, which is much larger, is not far off on the sands; and close by them are three or four houses, built in a row, which contain all the dwellers on the Point. These had a little garden, which was kept with great care, but few things would grow in such soil: there were some bright-looking wallflowers, I remember.

We soon found the lighthouse-keeper. He was a new man since our time, and could not at first understand how we had come, as the boats were not running.'

In 1878, it was a certain Richard Stead's turn to journey to Spurn. On page 94 of 'Holderness and the Holdernessians', published that year, he sets the scene in a chapter entitled 'A Day at Spurn'.

He took a dog cart from Patrington to Easington before he set foot on a sandy disorganized road leading to Kilnsea. By page 100 he observes that 'After a mile or two we began to find walking on the loose and apparently bottomless sand pretty hard work'. So he took to walking on the beach - 'We took to this firmer ground, of course, walking within a foot or two of the gently rippling wavelets, and found ourselves getting along much more satisfactorily.'

On arrival at Spurn he immediately visited the public house 'The Lifeboat Inn'. Mr Stead was surprised that a hostelry at such a remote location could be viable. He comments on page 102 'The average sale per week during summer, we were told, was from 60 to 100 gallons of draught beer, 40 dozen of bottled beer, 30 or 40 dozens of soda water, lemonade & etc, besides other things in no small quantities. There were fourteen families, besides one or two single men; in all 63 persons. Our surprise abated, however, when a little later on we saw a thirsty yachting party of twenty or so land, and make a descent on the hostelry. "It's visitors as duz it", we began to quite understand.'

But who were these visitors? The industrial

revolution may have forced many families into towns and cities where they worked long hours in harsh conditions, but it also gave them regular pay. With food prices static or even falling later in the 19th century, and manufactured goods steadily becoming more affordable due to mechanization and the increased division of labour, more people had a little spare money for leisure activities. After 1840, the railways rapidly opened up the country, and for the first time, the sea side resorts created by this new mode of transport were now within reach of town dwellers, many of whom had never seen the sea before! Indeed, some may never have been far from their own town or village, so the chance of a trip to Spurn Point would have seemed like an adventure to a desert island! And so, shop girls and clerks, machine workers, miners and mill hands set off from the industrial heartlands of West Yorkshire and Nottinghamshire clutching tickets for their expedition to unfamiliar shores.

So by the late 19th century, the excursion traffic from across the Humber was very well established, for the following entry is noted in the Spurn school log book on 23 May 1893 'Excursionists come in on Mondays and Thursday and I have heard that the girls were wanted at home earlier on those days than our 4 o'clock closing time. (Larry Malkin, Ann Stotham & Dorothy Smith - This peculiar and remote little school P4) The lifeboat men even earned a few extra coppers by conveying the holidaymakers, especially ladies, across the water to the waiting boats. (Jan Crowther – The People along the Sand P62)

Some of the visitors by this time were naturalists, and famous names such as Reverend Henry Slater; William Eagle Clarke; Reverend Edward Ponsonby Knubley: Francis Boyes and John Cordeaux regularly arrived at Spurn. Indeed, Cordeaux (1831 – 1899) lived at Great Coates on the South bank of the Humber, and began visiting Spurn in the late 1860s, when he usually arrived by boat. (Jan Crowther – The People along the Sand P59 - 61) From the 1880s onwards, there were naturalists' parties from Grimsby and Cleethorpes. When the Yorkshire Naturalists Union was founded, they also regularly visited in large groups to go down the peninsula, but even by the 1930s many naturalists did not go down Spurn due to difficulties. (P114)

Pubs

It might be wondered what brought visitors to Spurn in the 19th century. As noted above, many visitors were wild fowlers or studied nature; for others it was the opportunity to visit the lighthouse, but many came to enjoy the delights of several ale-houses in this remote place. Visitors travelling to Spurn by road in the mid 19th century would have passed two hostelries in Kilnsea – The Blue Bell and The Crown and Anchor. The Blue Bell was originally in Old Kilnsea, which was lost to the sea in the 1830s. It was rebuilt on its new site in 1847, with William Westerdale as the licensee. The Crown and Anchor was also rebuilt about 1852, after the demise of the old village, on a site even further away from the sea. The first landlord was Medforth Tennison. (Jan Crowther – The Alehouses of Spurn and Kilnsea)

Those venturing across from Lincolnshire had the chance to sample the offerings from the two public houses on the Point in the early 19th century – The Lifeboat Inn (sometimes called Mason's Arms) and The Tiger, which sold the cheaper beer! In 1822, Nixon James was listed as the victualler of this ale-house (Spurn Head Postal History R Ward 1988 P6), but he was superseded by John Thompson (who was the last lighthouse keeper to combine both duties), who was there on George Head's visit in 1835. As to The Lifeboat Inn, this public house had been built in part of the old Napoleonic barracks in the early 19th century. Much of its trade came from the crews of the gravel boats and fishing vessels that landed here. Robert Richardson was the victualler in 1822, and remained so until he retired in 1841, aged 55. (Spurn Head Postal History R Ward 1988 P10) By the time that the next publican took over The Lifeboat Inn, Joseph Davey, The Tiger seems to have disappeared from the scene. Davey only lasted until 1843, when Robert Brown took over. It was probably he who entertained Captain Bell and a select party of the pilot ship 'Neptune' in 1846. (Jan

Crowther - The People along the Sand P30) On October 1st 1846, Robert Brown, then master, asked for permission to erect a tenement for the accommodation of visitors from across the Humber from Cleethorpes. This was granted, but in 1848, his request to sell liquor on the beach was not, so he resigned. (Roy Benfell Spurn Lifeboat Station – The First Hundred Years P29 - 30) In 1849, Michael Welbourn became licensee, and he was probably the last coxswain to combine this with running the pub. (Jan Crowther – The People along the Sand P55). Further victuallers were John Quinton in 1871, and James Hopper in 1881, but by 1925 there was no mention in any directory of an innkeeper at Spurn Point. (Roy Benfell Spurn Lifeboat Station – The First Hundred Years P11 - 13)

Post Office

It is not surprising that the influx of visitors ultimately let to the establishment of the Post Office on Spurn in the mid 19th century, but prior to that, the peninsula was home to an earlier form of communication. An optical telegraph was installed in September 1839, with links to Hull via the Sand Light off Spurn – Grimsby – Killingholme, and then Paull. This survived until 1857 when Cleethorpes took over the Spurn role of notifying shipping movements. (Spurn Head Postal History R Ward 1988 P9) It was eventually replaced by the electric telegraph on January 25th 1871. (Roy Benfell Spurn Lifeboat Station – The First Hundred Years P43) A telephone was installed in the master's house in October 1893.

On July 31st 1868, two men visited in connection with the possibility of establishing a post office there. This was sanctioned by the Post Master General on August 5th, when Eliza Hopper, born 1849, became the first sub-postmistress, and in fact the only one throughout its entire existence on Spurn! (Roy Benfell Spurn Lifeboat Station – The First Hundred Years P105 - 106) The electric telegraph mentioned above was in the charge of Eliza Hopper after it was installed. The P.O. was located in the Coxwain's house.

Barney Coy was the resident postman from 1871 to 1906 when at the age of 68 he retired (Jan

Crowther – The People along the Sand P48), and he was replaced by Mr Moore, who had a hut for his sole use, just inside the fort, for letters and grocery lists. (Ronald Kendall Growing up on Spurn Head P34) The post office closed not long after the First World War, in about 1920. By 1925 there was no mention on Spurn of the inn and P.O. (Spurn Head Postal History R Ward 1988 P13), so it would appear that they both ceased at the same time.

The rapid growth in picture postcards from 1894 until their decline after WW1 must have been a real boon to the Spurn post office, and many examples of postcards with its distinctive franking still exist. Excursionists were eager to send a memento home of their exploits! Additionally, the militarization of the point in 1914 brought considerable trade to both P.O. and the Lifeboat Inn. It is hardly surprising then that the winding down of Green Battery on the Point in 1919 led ultimately to the loss of both facilities.

Traders

Not all the traffic at Spurn was inward bound, for the 'Market boat' took crabs to market at Grimsby when the men on Spurn had enough, usually once a week. (George A Jarratt Memories of Spurn in the 1880s P11) Often the residents of Spurn would take a boat to Grimsby with a shopping list, especially near Christmas. Water was even brought from Grimsby when the rainwater tanks on the Spurn houses ran low! (Roy Benfell Spurn Lifeboat Station – The First Hundred Years P32) Records exist of a number of traders who visited this remote location as part of their everyday activities. Provisions arrived courtesy of Mr Webster of Easington, and Eric Keyworth, butcher, who went to Spurn on Saturday with his horse and cart. Fresh milk was brought from John Clubley's farm at Easington by Mr Sharp with his pony and trap daily. (Ronald Kendall Growing up on Spurn Head P33 - 34) It is recorded that a greengrocer from as far away as Welwick traded there in the 1880s. (Jan Crowther – The People along the Sand P39) Robinson Webster and Albert Clubley provided the groceries to Spurn after 1905 on Wednesdays. (Jan Crowther – The People along the Sand P73)

We leave the last word on the visitors to Mr Kendall, who grew up on the Point in the 1920s. He remembered;

'During these summer days, trippers came over from Cleethorpes. They came in small boats dressed over all. They came four or five at a time to look out for each other and returned the same way because of the dangerous tides running at the mouth of the Humber. They would embark between the Pier and the Lifeboat House. They were assisted ashore on running planks by one or two of the Lifeboat Men. The boats would then stand just off the beach, moored to each other until the passengers were all ready to go back again. As trippers embarked, the hat was passed round each boat in turn. When all were safely aboard they would head back to Cleethorpes.

Sea holly was sold all at 1d or 2d a bunch. Most of lifeboat women supplied tea to trippers.

Mother would put a sign outside the porch door and prepare a table and chairs to accommodate them. This practice was stopped before the Second World War and has never been resumed.' (Ronald Kendall Growing up on Spurn Head P49)

Images in this book by kind permission of :
P17, P18, P19, P21, P22, P25, P26, P27, P28, P29, P30, P31, P32, P33, P34, P35, P36, P37, P40, P41, P42, P43, P61 Courtesy of Liz Betts, Barton upon Humber.
P15, P16, P65, P66, P67, P68, P71 Courtesy of Jenny Cartwright, Grimsby Library.
P78, P79, P80 Courtesy of Peter & Jan Crowther, Kilnsea.
P72 Courtesy of Roland Stork, Bridlington.
P77 Courtesy of John Kettley, Easington.
P91, P92, P95, P96, P97, P98 Courtesy of Torkel Larsen, Withernsea.
P48 Courtesy of Nigel Land, Barton upon Humber.
P93 Courtesy of Chris Hemery, Withernsea.
P81, P82 Courtesy of Hull Daily Mail/MEN Media.
P83 Courtesy of Yorkshire Wildlife Trust, Spurn Visitor Centre.

All other images are the author's own collection.

Image from 'Jackson's Guide to Grimsby Docks, Cleethorpes, & Neighbourhood' c1880, showing the tip of Spurn Point.

Image from 'Jackson's Guide to Grimsby Docks, Cleethorpes & Neighbourhood', showing Victorian ladies in bustles enjoying a walk with their partners near Smeaton's Lighthouse on Spurn c1880.

Should you choose to walk to Spurn from Easington in 1900, The Blue Bell Inn, Kilnsea, was there to fortify you as you started the hard 4 mile walk along sand.

A party of excursionists outside the Lifeboat Inn, the building on the left, Spurn c1900.

The precarious position of the Lifeboat Inn, Spurn, on a stormy day can be seen in this postcard c1900.

This postcard c1900 show the 1895 lighthouse, the lifeboat cottages, with the the right hand end cottage by then the P.O. and the school house on the extreme right.

This looks like a family outing at Spurn, sitting in a fishing boat at the turn of the last century. The lifeboat cottages are behind them.

An alternative use for a fishing boat recorded on an Edwardian postcard!

An Edwardian postcard with an image from 1829. It shows the Smeaton lighthouse and the 1816 low light, built on the seaward side.

13/8/13.

My dear Mother,
           Just a view of the L'
house. 100 years ago. It
has changed my word.
We tried to go up it yesterday
but it is closed to the public
on account of suffragettes.
I am very well and enjoying
myself. Hope to see you
and Bell soon. We have
been on the sands every day.
but it has turned out wet
this morning so thought it
best to stop in. I am quite
tanned what with camp.
and sea air. They are all
looking A1. and I am taking
care of them. Trust you are
all A1. W. L. Trevr.

Mrs. F.E. Montague Huggins
18 De Grey Rd.
Leeds

The back of the postcard on the previous page. Obviously the suffragettes were creating a problem for visitors to the lighthouse in 1913!

24

The Coastguard Station, Spurn, depicted on another Edwardian postcard, with the new lighthouse of 1895 in the background.

With the Lifeboat Inn in the distance, we see the mortuary in the centre and the lighthouse keepers' dwellings on the right. They originally surrounded the Smeaton light that was taken down in 1895.

Another picture postcard c1900, showing a visiting party using the coastguards' telescope.

A delightful image of excursionists, c 1910, rushing off the tender boat that ferried them to the beach from one of the paddle steamers.

Edwardian gentlemen at leisure on the Point, outside a makeshift shelter!

Crabbing, Spurn-style for these lads in the early 20th century!

Fishing as well by local lads at the time. The Humber keel in the background is engaged on the Spurn gravel trade, which took place on the Stony Binks outside the Point.

Spurn lifeboat men at their look-out post on the seaward side, opposite their cottages.

A winkle competition in the early 20th century. Which children are locals and which are visitors we do not know.

Using a boat as a vantage point over a century ago.

Fishing cobles, with the mausoleum in the background. The gentleman in the uniform was Consitt Hopper, the Lloyd's agent on Spurn Point.

Trader with cart c1900. They have probably travelled down from Easington via the beach.

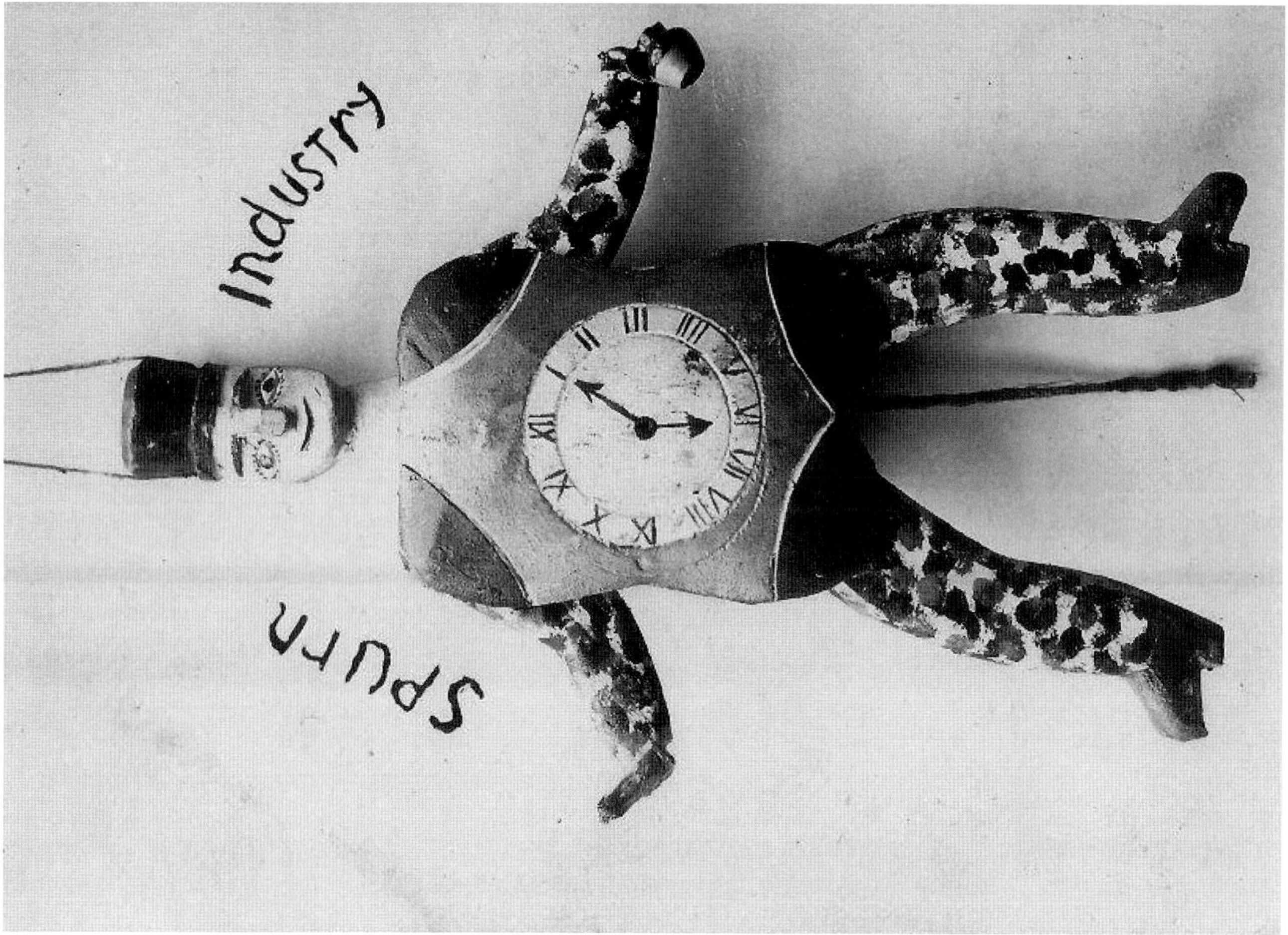
Industry
Spurn

38

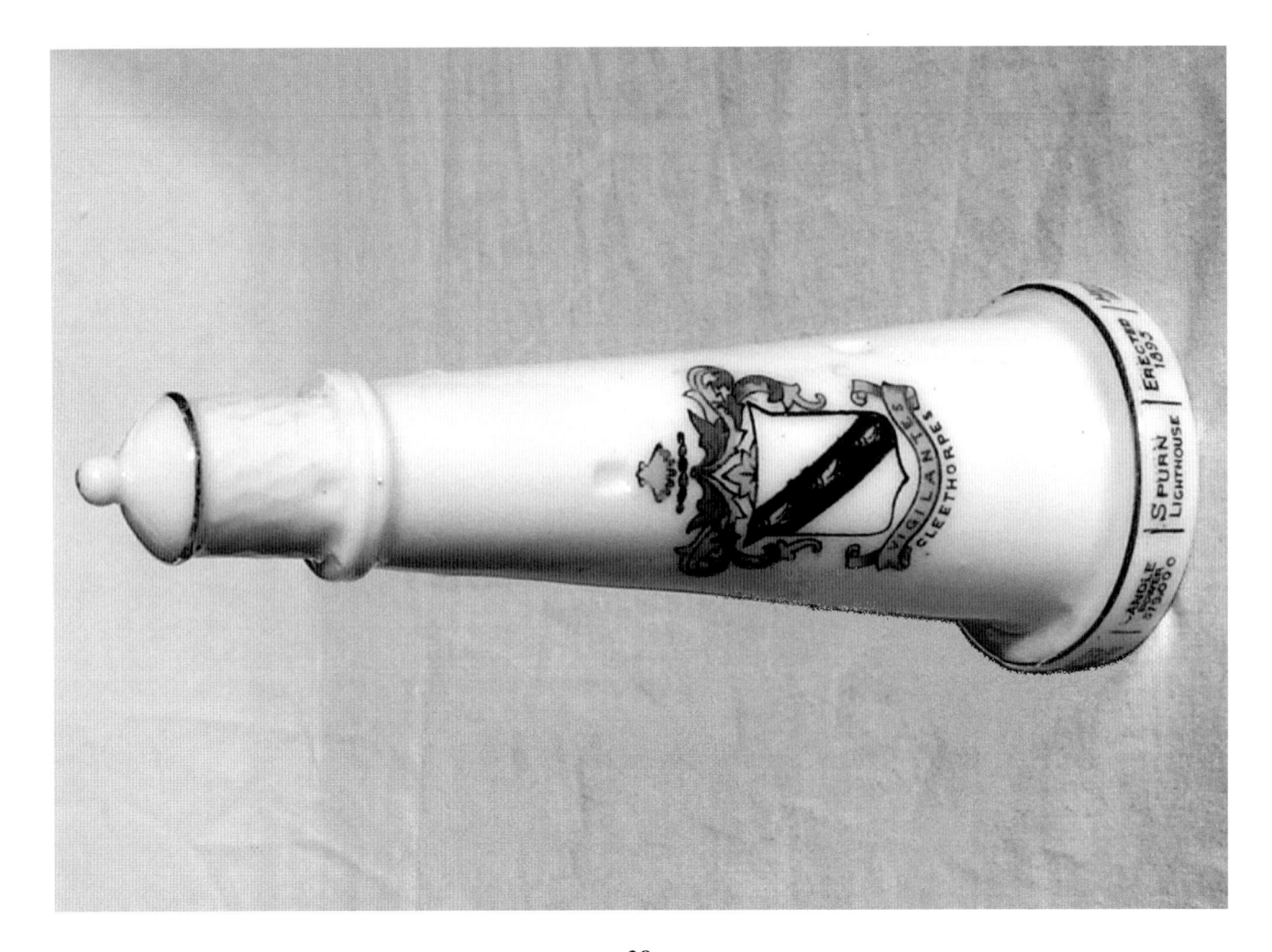

39

Lighthouse Spurn Head

OLD LOW LIGHT, SPURN
LISTER'S SERIES 36

Reflectors, Low Light, Spurn.
Lister's Series 632.

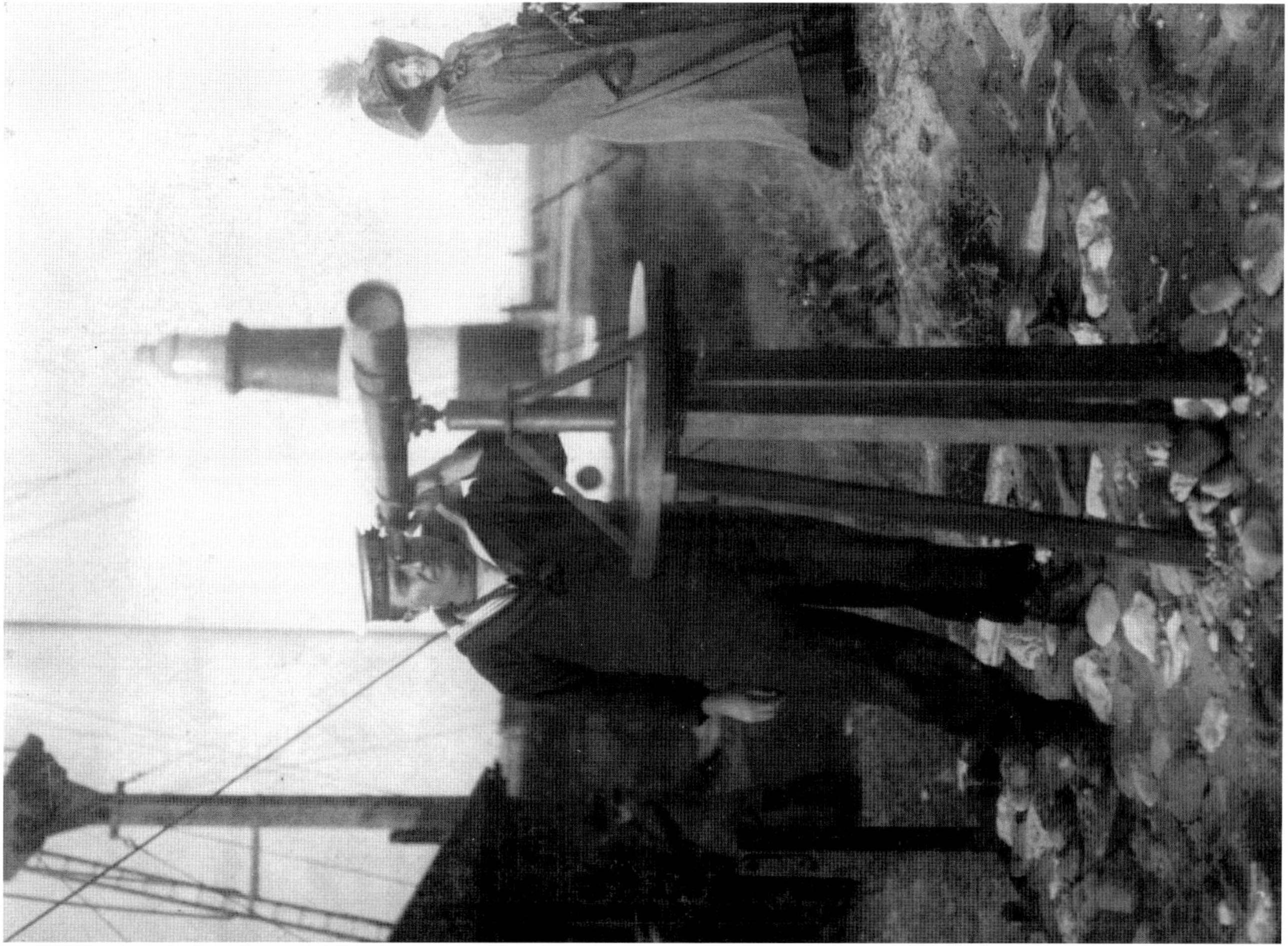

Descriptions for images on pages 37 to 43

Page 37. A rather curious Spurn postcard c1900. Between 1894 and the closure of the Post Office in 1920, many thousands of postcards were dispatched from both sides of the Humber.

Page 38. A porcelain model of Spurn Lighthouse, bearing the Cleethorpes crest. Many such tourist trinkets were sold during the heyday of excursion travel to Spurn.

Page 39. A rather blurred but delightful postcard of a party of day trippers - probably a school outing. A visit round the lighthouse was always popular, and the lighthouse keepers usually welcomed the visitors, as it helped pass the time in this remote location.

Page 40. A picture of the Smeaton lighthouse of 1776. Supported by buttresses, and taken just before it was due to be replaced by Thomas Matthew's lighthouse in 1895.

Page 41. A postcard of the Spurn's last low lighthouse. It was built in 1852, being decommisioned when Matthew's new lighthouse became operational in 1895.

Page 42. A very scarce postcard of the reflectors from the last low light at Spurn. Postcards of the reflectors of the high lighthouse are more common.

Page 43. A superb image from the collection of Liz Betts of Barton on Humber. One of the Spurn coastguards is busy doing his job while an admiring female excursionist in all her Edwardian finery looks on.

Sailing Boats

Many tourists came across to Spurn in boats provided by local fishermen from Grimsby and Cleethorpes, usually small schooners capable of holding perhaps thirty visitors. The railway then built the pier in 1873, and added a landing stage in 1875 for these craft to exploit the trade. Unfortunately, this addition was destroyed by fire in 1886, but the boats, powered by nothing more than oars and sail, continued to ply their trade well into the twentieth century. By then, boats with names such as 'Silver Foam' and 'Violet' had been joined by motor craft.

Edward Dobson's 'A guide and directory to Cleethorpes with an historical account of the place, to which is appended a perpetual tide table shewing the proper time for sea-bathing, according to the moon's age…. Etc' Written and compiled by Edward Dobson, Cleethorpes, July 1850 adds the following section;-

'From the highest part of Cliff Terrace is a sloping road of artificial steps, leading to the oyster booth of Mr William Rowston, which is situate at the bottom. Near to this booth are pleasure boats in readiness to take out parties to Spurn, or pleasure excursions into the Humber, or German Ocean, when required; they are neat little vessels, with 'lug sails', safe, and well adapted for the purpose'.

On page 21 and 22 of John Heywood's Illustrated Guide to Grimsby and Cleethorpes 1890;

'Boating facilities are in plenty, either for rowing or sailing. The boating, close in shore, is much more pleasant than formerly, the new sea wall having effected a vast improvement, by stopping the constant washing away of the cliffs, and consequent accumulation of mud. Sailing boats of large size, schooner-rigged, are provided for short runs out to sea, or excursions to Spurn Point.

Ward's Cleethorpes and District Illustrated Guide for 1900 notes on page 29;

'There is no safer boating in England that what can be had at Cleethorpes, the boats being in charge of hard and well-tried fishermen, who have shown their true British pluck on more than one occasion by going out in their row boats to the rescue of shipwrecked crews, many of whom have had their deeds of daring suitably rewarded by the Royal Humane Society and may often be seen wearing the medals awarded them…. A favourite trip is to Spurn Point; this may be made by steamer or schooner, the former leaves Grimsby and the latter Cleethorpes during the season, time of sailing varies according to the tide. A visit to the lighthouse and its environs are very interesting.'

After this date, the Cleethorpes guides are increasingly full of the pleasures of a Humber crossing on the paddle steamers rather than by sail. If we look at the Cleethorpes Council Meeting minutes for the period after the First World War, there is still considerable mention of the sailing craft, but this naturally diminishes as the years pass by. The notes for May 7th 1918 mention licences granted to Pleasure boats 'Grace Darling' and 'Fern', but by 1924 a problem seemed to be presenting itself in the guise of plying for trade on a Sunday. Here is how the entry for January 24th chronicles the dispute: 'Further considered petition from 11 boatmen (out of 62 licensed boatmen) asking that Sunday boating be allowed. Also considering resolution from leaders of Cleethorpes Wesleyan Church asking Council not to grant further facilities for Sunday boating. Committee recommended that Sunday boating be not allowed.' The matter did not rest there, for on August 13th, there is another petition from some boat owners to allow Sunday pleasure boat trips. This was turned down again.

However, the rebuttals of 1924 did not prevent the Sunday issue from raising its head again in 1925. The minutes of April 28th records that 'The Sands Committee recommended that prohibition against boating (plying for hire by licensed boatmen) on Sunday be removed. This was followed on May 19th by 'Licensing Committee – recommended that Council do not adopt recommendation of Sands Committee that Sunday boating be allowed (Council agreed with Licensing Committee 20 May 1925). In usual Council fashion, a compromise was sought at the June 9th meeting 'Licensing Committee –

Cleethorpes Pleasure Boatmen's Association asked that the question of Sunday boating be reconsidered. Committee recommended that clause prohibiting Sunday boating be deleted from licence of those owners who gave written undertaking not to tout for passengers on Sunday.' I am confident that in the long term the Sunday clause vanished and boat owners plied their trade each and every day!

The council had other boating matters to consider in 1925, for one of the boatmen, a certain Mr G Broddle, was receiving complaints from his customers. The first is mentioned on July 22nd 'Complaint from visitor re Mr Broddle – took 2 seats @ 3/6 per head on his boat 'Silver Foam' for journey to Spurn and stay there of 1 hour – after being taken a few miles the boat returned without landing at Spurn.' This was followed on August 13th by another grievance 'Further complaint against Mr G Broddle re insulting language to lady who accompanied the person who previously complained that Mr Broddle had taken passengers in his boat on the promise to land them at Spurn and had subsequently refused to land them. Mr B summoned to the meeting of Licensing committee and informed that if any further complaint his licence would be suspended.' What became of Mr Broddle we do not know, for he is not mentioned again that year!

A final tit-bit in this chapter regards the licensing of pleasure craft in 1927. On July 20th and 25th, the minutes note '7 boats to be allowed to ply for hire to Spurn (new condition annexed to Licence that boats should not go outside 3 mile limit). It would appear that by this time, probably for safety reasons, some of the craft were limited to sea-trips of less than three miles from Cleethorpes. By 1927, the paddle steamers 'Solway' and 'Humber' had gone, and increasingly, the cross-Humber traffic from Grimsby and Cleethorpes to Spurn was by motor craft. Any visit by paddle steamer was now by L.N.E.R. ships seconded from the Hull to New Holland crossing. It is very unlikely that these vessels landed passengers actually on the Point.

A scarce late 19th century image of folk at Cleethorpes queuing up for a trip across the Humber to Spurn aboard the sailing boat, 'Quickstep'.

Cleethorpes actively promoted Spurn Point as a destination, as can be seen in this Edwardian postcard with Spurn lighthouse the centre piece. It was far easier to travel to Spurn via Cleethorpes, which had a railway.

Cleethorpes Pier c1910, with the landing stage for the sailing schooners to cross the Humber. I'm assured by a learned friend that the boat is actually a ketch though!

Having travelled across the Humber to Spurn in a sailing boat, excursionists just might get their feet wet when disembarking!

Paddle Steamers

Steam packets had arrived on the river, running between Hull and Gainsborough, as early as 1814, but the first recorded excursion to Spurn was run by the Grimsby and Hull Steam Packet Company, using two of its ferries, the 'Kingston', built 1828, and 'Pelham', built 1832. Both were in operation during the summer of 1832, offering potential travellers the chance to leave Hull at approximately 7 a.m., call at Grimsby between 9.00 and 10.00 a.m. and sail onward to Spurn. The trippers returned in the evening, and the charge for this wonderful day out was 'Best Cabin, one shilling and sixpence' or 'Fore Cabin, just one shilling'!

In the summer of 1840, two ferries built in 1836, the 'Don' and 'John Bull', commenced trips from as far away as Thorne! Owned by the Thorne Packet Company, they charged three shillings from the town, and two shillings from Hull for the very long journey out to Spurn Point. Coaches were even provided from Doncaster to feed into the service, starting at the ungodly hour of 5 a.m.! Initially these boat trips proved popular, but competition from the railways eventually ended the traffic from the West Riding in 1856. However, the destination obviously continued to be desirable as in 1843, Robert Brown, the Master of the Spurn lifeboat, asked for and was granted permission to build accommodation for the many visitors from across the river. The Hull to New Holland route, introduced in the 1820s, started to provide paddle steamers for the excursion traffic, the earliest recorded being 1865, but their use was to continue until after World War 2. A personal memory of these visits is in George Jarratt's booklet 'Memories of Spurn in the 1880s'. On page 9 he records that 'Occasionally, in the finest weather in summer, the paddle-wheel tugboat trippers brought trippers from Hull and were landed by fishing boats for about an hour. The first ice-cream I ever tasted was when a man who had come down with the tug-boat, carried his small freezer, complete, to the cottages and we were allowed a penny-worth each, in a cup.'

The arrival of the Manchester, Sheffield and Lincolnshire Railway into Cleethorpes in

1863 had created a new seaside resort, and the opportunity for trippers to brave the mere seven miles across the estuary to land on the point. With the rapid expansion of trippers to Cleethorpes in the late Victorian and Edwardian era, the lucrative business of ferrying them to Spurn was provided by the two paddle steamers best known for this journey – the 'Solway' and 'Humber'. (Lloyd's Registers 1897 to 1927) Both started their lives as paddle tugs, 'Solway', of 103 tons gross, being built in 1886 by Ramage & Ferguson of Leith for the North British Steam Packet Company for use at Port Carlisle, Silloth. She arrived at Grimsby in 1897 and was owned by Thomas Copeland of that town. With a dark funnel, probably black, and a light coloured mid stripe, she was soon appearing on postcards of the time. 'The 'Humber', originally named 'William Stephenson', constructed at the South Shields yard of J T Eltringham in 1895, was slightly larger at 131 tons gross, and sported a pale coloured funnel. Initially she worked on the Tyne at North Shields, but sailed to her new owner, James Turner, of Cleethorpes in 1901. Whereas the schooners set sail to Spurn from the beach at Cleethorpes, both paddle steamers plied their trade from Grimsby Docks, near the tower. From the word go they were very successful, carrying about three hundred trippers at a time across the estuary. However, the regular paddle ships were not the only steamers operating on the Humber, for a certain steam leisure craft 'Mrytle', from Hull, required lifeboat assistance back to Grimsby on September 1st 1878. (Roy Benfell - Spurn Lifeboat Station; The First Hundred Years, page 118)

The steamers made their journeys on Mondays and Thursdays, when handbills were handed out on the promenade at Cleethorpes to advertise the service. There were often fishing competitions on this short passage, and to ensure that the tourists didn't get their feet wet on disembarking, small boats called tenders would transport them to the beach on the river side of the point. Once there, they could visit and inspect the new lighthouse, opened in 1895, view the lifeboat, or purchase teas and cakes from the lifeboatmen's wives, who took it in turns to earn some very welcome extra pennies. Back then, there was a school at

'Spurn Village' and on these days during the season, the children would leave early to help their mothers with this trade, and Abel Heywood & Son's Glade Books – 'A Guide to Cleethorpes & Grimsby 1909' is effusive about the virtues of a trip across the Humber. It contains the following long section on pages 12 & 13, under the heading 'Spurn Point'.

'A most interesting excursion is to Spurn Point with its new lighthouse (built 1895) and beautiful beach. Roomy and comfortable steamers start from Grimsby and reach the point in about an hour, and usually give the visitor about three hours on the headland. The landing is generally made by means of a small boat, and the visitor finds himself in a small village consisting of a row of cottages built upon a narrow strip of land, washed by the sea on three sides. Tea may be had at several of the cottages.

The lighthouse is 120 feet high. Its great flash is visible for a distance of 17 miles, it is white and shows for two seconds, and is eclipsed for eighteen seconds. The old lighthouse was built in 1773 by Smeaton, the builder of the famous Eddystone lighthouse, and did duty for 120 years.

The voyager to Spurn Point (distance seven miles) will sail over the water which now covers the Port of Ravenserodd, once a formidable rival to Grimsby. In the reign of Edward the First, allusion is made to this port in a record called "Veredictum de Grymsby in Lindsey" a kind of report of which we would call now-a-days a commission of enquiry. It states the condition of Grymsby as a demesne royal, and goes on to say that the burgesses have a Charter of King Henry, father of the king, for transacting commerce and other matters. It is said that about eleven years previously, or something more, the sea bed cast up much mud and stone, and that with this accumulation, William de Fortiter, the Earl of Albemarle, had begun to build a certain town called Ravenserodd, which is an island, inasmuch, as the sea surrounds it, and it is damaging the town of Grymsby and the country generally. They also say "the men of the said town of Ravenserodd sail with the vessels bringing merchants ware and making for the

Port of Grymsby with these wares and carry them by force to Ravenserodd." Ravenserodd (sometimes called Ravenspurne and Ravenser) was a borough as well as a seaport, and sent in 1350 two members to Edward the Third's Parliament, and in 1360 three members were returned. In the year 1399 (23rd of Richard the Second), Ravenserodd became famous as the place at which the Duke of Lancaster, afterwards Henry the Fourth, landed from France, and was joined by the Earls of Northumberland and Westmoreland and others.

"The banished Bolingbroke repeals himself,
And with uplifted arms is safe arrived
At Ravenspurg"

In the Annals of England, by William of Worcester, it is stated that John of Gaunt died in February 1399, and that the Duke of Hereford and Lancaster landed about the Feast of St. John the Baptist (29th August) at Ravenspur, and "equitavit apud Bristollium" – rode to Bristol – and there beheaded William Scrope, Earl of Wiltshire, the King's Treasurer, and afterwards rode to the Castle of Flentt (Flint), where the king was, and brought him to London in September. The sword which Henry wore on landing at Ravenspurne is now in the Tower of London. "Trinity sands" are pointed out to excursionists, as the spot where this once important seaport flourished.' Incidentally, the historical note that in 1360 three members of parliament were returned is inaccurate, as the last trading in the seaport was actually 1358!

The Cleethorpes Guide of 1914, on page 23, described the chance to visit Spurn by paddle steamer:

'Sea Trips – a trip on the briny possesses charms for most holiday makers, and there is no lack of facilities for them to indulge their bent at Cleethorpes, for pleasure steamers leave almost daily during the season for excursions along the Yorkshire and Lincolnshire Coasts to Hull, Scarborough, Mablethorpe, Spurn, etc. Many of the steamers carry fishing tackle, and passengers often amuse themselves with fishing competitions during the trip. Most of the vessels also carry entertainers of some sort who provide harmony and diversion.'

The Great War changed this idyllic scene. The boats returned after the conflict, but 'Solway' moved on in 1922 to Jarrow on the Tyne. 'Humber' lasted until 1926, when she was broken up. However, the sailing boats, and the new fangled motor launches remained. By now, the L.N.E.R. had taken over the Humber ferries, and the Cleethorpes Council Meeting minutes of November 22nd 1937 noted 'LNER River Cruises operate daily from the Grimsby Docks during the summer months.' The Cleethorpes Guide of 1939 reiterates this on page 6 'Regular steamer sailings from the Pier head and Royal Dock, Grimsby (LNER). Afternoon and evening trips.' The excursions continued to Spurn after WW2, though by then they no longer landed trippers on the Point.

The leaflets of the time mention 'musical selections' being played onboard, and the fare from Grimsby, Royal Dock Basin in 1939 was one shilling to Spurn, two shillings to Hull, and even as far as Withernsea for two shillings and sixpence! The boats best known for this traffic were the 'Killingholme', and 'Brocklesby', both built in 1912 and scrapped in 1945.

After nationalization, British Railways continued the excursions, often starting from Hull, sporadically into the 1970s, using the later paddle steamers 'Tattershall Castle', 'Wingfield Castle' & 'Lincoln Castle'. The late Alan Dowling, of Cleethorpes, observed that the Humber cruises in 1950s and 1960s sailed from Grimsby Tidal Basin, just outside the lock gates, not from the actual dock itself. The withdrawal of the New Holland ferry in 1981 brought this traffic to an end. The age of the paddle steamer was over.

Page 58 image. A poster advertising an outing on P.S. 'Pelham' from Hull in 1832.(Alan Dowling - Cleethorpes ; The Creation of a Seaside Resort, Phillimore 2005, page 15)

Page 67 image. 1939 advert in the Cleethorpes Holiday Annual, advertising trips from Grimsby with the London & North Eastern Railway. By this time the boats would be P.S. Brocklesby and P.S. Killingholme.

Page 68 image. A similar advert in the 1947 Cleethorpes Holiday Guide. P.S. 'Tattershall Castle', Wingfield Castle' and 'Lincoln Castle' were in operation after 1945.

EXCURSION
OF THE
STEAM PACKET
PELHAM
TO SEA,
CALLING AT SPURN.

On THURSDAY, the 30th instant, the above Packet, Capt. WATERLAND, will leave HULL at Half-past Eight in the Morning, and GRIMSBY at Half-past Ten, on an Excursion to Sea, calling at Spurn, to return in the Evening.

THE PROPRIETORS most respectfully return thanks to their Friends and the Public for the many favours conferred upon them during the last four years, and earnestly solicit a continuance of their decided preference in favour of the Pelham; assuring them that every means in their power shall be used to merit the support so extensively expressed on their behalf.

Best Cabin, 1s. 6d.—Fore Cabin, 1s.

T. Wintringham.

GRIMSBY, 20th August, 1832.

SKELTON, PRINTER, GRIMSBY.

A superb early 20th century postcard of the paddle steamer 'Humber' leaving Grimsby, packed with tourists. The P.S. 'Solway' is berthed on the right.

A postcard of the paddle steamer 'Humber' mid river. Standing room only!

A postcard depicting the tender, or 'coggy boat' of the P.S. 'Humber.' ferrying excursionists to the beach at Spurn.

Another view of passengers being conveyed to the shore at Spurn, this time from the P.S. 'Solway'.

Ready to go ashore, the paddle steamer has gone perilously close to the beach. A sailing boat awaits the return of its day trippers.

A rather poor but scarce image of the P.S.'Solway' berthed at Grimsby. Fewer pictures of P.S.'Solway' than P.S.'Humber' seem to have survived. The 'Humber' had a light coloured funnel, whereas the 'Solway' had a dark funnel with a light coloured mid band. The caption mirrors the one on the 'Cynicus' postcard which is printed on the back board of this book.

An advert from the Grimsby & Cleethorpes Guide c1905 promoting the service provided by the paddle steamer 'Solway'.

The PASSENGER STEAMERS

HUMBER
AND
SOLWAY

Will make Excursions from the

Grimsby Tower

TO

SPURN.

Every MONDAY & THURSDAY

FOR FURTHER PARTICULARS
SEE HANDBILLS & POSTERS.

Also to HULL,

WEATHER AND TIDE PERMITTING.

J. WEBSTER,
Family Butcher.

—Only the Finest Quality of—
English Beef and Mutton sold.

FAMILIES AND SHIPPING SUPPLIED.
PICKLED TONGUES & CORNED BEEF.

NOTE THE ADDRESS:
Corner of Sea View & Bancroft Street.
Branch—MARKET PLACE.

John Osborne,

FOOD PROVIDER,

VIENNA BREAD BAKER,

AND CONFECTIONER,

36 & 37 Alexandra Road,
and **4 Brighton Street**
Opposite the Fountain on the New King's Parade.

Established 1873. **CLEETHORPES**

FRUIT PIES for Dinner a Speciality.
Provision Merchant & Importer of Danish Produce.

A page from the Grimsby & Cleethorpes Guide of 1906 / 7, advertising the excursions from Grimsby provided by both paddle steamers.

DAILY RIVER CRUISES

By L.N.E.R.
PADDLE STEAMER

FROM

Royal Dock Basin

GRIMSBY

THROUGHOUT THE SEASON

(Weather and other circumstances permitting)

To
- SPURN - - 1/-
- HULL - - 2/-
- WITHERNSEA - 2/6
- READS ISLAND 2/6

(According to Programme)

MUSICAL SELECTIONS WILL BE PLAYED ON BOARD THE STEAMER DURING THESE CRUISES

LICENSED BUFFET AND LIGHT REFRESHMENTS ON BOARD.

For further particulars of Cruises, see handbills at Stations, or apply to L.N.E.R. Marine Dept, Dock Offices, Grimsby.

A frequent train service is in operation between Cleethorpes and Grimsby Docks, and a special omnibus service down the Royal Dock to alongside the Ferry Steamer.

Passengers by these cruises have an opportunity of seeing the Royal Dock and shipping. In addition, passengers desiring to ascend the Dock Tower (300 ft. high), at the lock entrance to Grimsby Docks, can do so (subject to the exigencies of the docking of vessels at tide time) upon application at the Dock Master's Office adjoining the Tower. The charge for this facility is 6d. per head (children half-price) in parties of not less than four.

Daily River Cruises

BY LNER

PADDLE STEAMER

FROM

ROYAL DOCK BASIN GRIMSBY

THROUGHOUT THE SEASON

(Weather and other circumstances permitting)

TO

SPURN HULL READS ISLAND etc.

LICENSED BUFFET AND LIGHT REFRESHMENTS ON BOARD

For further particulars of Cruises, see press advertisements, or apply to LNER Marine Department, Dock Offices, Grimsby, or Local Stations

A frequent train service is in operation between Cleethorpes & Grimsby Docks

Motor Craft

The introduction of motorized craft was a natural progression on from sail and steam, and initially caused great friction with the older sailors, and two early boats licensed by the local authorities, the 'Coralie' and 'Silver Spray', were effectively pushed out of the business by bullying tactics from the older fraternity! However, by the late 1920s, motor craft were accepted and joined in this profitable trade.

The rise of motor craft in the Cleethorpes to Spurn trade can be deduced from the minutes of Cleethorpes Council Meeting. The notes for the meeting of October 7th 1919 mention licences granted for the previous year; 8 Boats, 8 Boatmen, Motor Boats 0. However, the listing for 1919 has the following tally: Boats 20, 36 Boatmen, 4 Motor Boats. The age of the internal combustion engine was making its impact felt on the Spurn leisure trade. By 1920 the figures were: Boats 41, Boatmen 51, Motor Boats 9.

The minutes for May 31st 1920 state that licences were granted to 24 pleasure boats – carrying from 4 to 18 passengers. The notes for the July 15th 1931 council meeting show that 19 motor boats and 15 boatmen now had licences. Obviously, motor boats were now very much in the ascendancy. The 1930 Cleethorpes Guide noted that these motor boats 'landing at Spurn, subject to tide'. The Guide for 1939 adds further detail on page 6 - 'Motor boats under fully licensed men ply for hire on the South, Central and North Beaches. A number of speed boats are also available.'

Returning to the minutes of Cleethorpes Council Meetings, we find that between 1936 and 1940, N Blow & Co (Oberon Cruising Co. Ltd) were granted the privilege of embarking and disembarking passengers on the pierhead landing stage from their vessel 'White Lady II' for the 1936, 1937, 1938 and 1939 seasons. (NELA 51/1/37, Pier etc Cleethorpes committee 15 May 1936 and 19 October 1936). However, the company decided in April 1939 not to operate vessels during the coming season. (NELA

51/1/40, pier etc Committee 3 April 1939). By May 18th 1939, the licences issued were now: 10 motor boats, 1 rowing boat and 12 boatmen. On June 7th, there was a complaint against the pleasure vessel 'Sunbeam' (licensee G Holmes). The owner was allowed to explain, and the council appear to have accepted his account.

As to the final licences before World War 2, the seasonal licenses were due to expire on July 19th. The following licences were issued on September 30th 1939 – 8 motor pleasure boats, 1 rowing boat, 13 boatmen, with an additional licence granted to a solitary boatman just before this date. One can safely assume that none of these craft would now land 'subject to tide' on the heavily militarized Green Battery at Spurn Point. The days of personal landings at the peninsula were over.

The only image that I have seen of an early motor powered boat on the Cleethorpes to Spurn leisure trade. The date is probably the mid 1920s and is taken from 'The Grimsby Telegraph' dated 13 / 2 / 2010.

A rather poor photograph taken on a box brownie camera in 1935. Another scarce scene, this time of a commercial motor cruiser at Spurn.

The Railway and Sail Power

The Spurn military railway was constructed during WW1, in order to facilitate the fortification of the Green Battery on Spurn Point and the Godwin Battery at Kilnsea. Initially, steam engines were used, but petrol rail cars were soon introduced to handle conveyance of personnel. For full details of this fascinating railway, read Howard Frost's excellent publication 'Sailing the Rails: A New History of Spurn and its Military Railway'. From the very beginning, the local postman had obviously availed himself of this new facility, as the Spurn school diary for November 5th 1915 notes 'Again on Friday, the mail train was so late…. I could not mark the registers.' This was noted by Vincent G Skelton, who was the teacher at this unique school at the time. (Spurn Head Postal History R Ward 1988, page 16) When, after 1919 the line saw considerably less use, the local residents saw an opportunity!

The first mention of using sail power as a means of transport on the Spurn Point military railway was reported in the 'Hull Daily Mail', dated October 5th 1922. It would appear that two local residents of Kilnsea, a Mr Charles Hailes and Mr Edwin Hodgson, struck upon the idea when they needed to get down the peninsula in a hurry. They found a redundant bogie and utilised a discarded sheet that had been used as a cinema screen in the YMCA hut at the artillery garrison for the sail. The prototype underwent a number of changes, and between the wars, there appear to have been several of these sail bogies created. They were used mostly by the lifeboatmen, lighthouse keepers and any visiting civilians, which was something of a liberty, as after all, this was a military railway under the ultimate jurisdiction of the army!

This is how the Hull Daily Mail described this unusual mode of transport in its original article:

HULL DAILY MAIL OCTOBER 5TH 1922
THE ONLY WAY

The ordinary road from Patrington to Withernsea is, of course, impossible. Hardly anyone ventures this way nowadays unless he is asking for broken springs and other damage. The only way is to turn off to the left down Preston Long-Lane (just before entering Preston) to Lelley, and to proceed via Burton Pidsea and Roos whether one is making for Patrington or Withernsea. We have been over this road several times lately, and find it, too, is getting potholey in places, and after rain there are some swampy corners. Still it is tolerably good going, but the road is narrow, and users should be on the lookout for the large cars which are using this route.

MAKING FOR SPURN

On reaching Patrington we decided to push on to as near Spurn as possible. The road took us through Welwick, Skeffling, Easington and Kilnsea, but we are not going to assume the responsibility of advising any motorists to go over it. Anyway, there were compensations for we heard the great story of the "landship", and enjoyed a novel experience.

GO BY "LANDSHIP"

Between Kilnsea and Spurn is a stretch of three miles of sands and grassy dunes, and it makes very rough walking indeed; the tide has also to be taken into consideration. Walking, nowadays, though, is not necessary. You go by landship, which daily conveys to and fro, officers and men at the battery, lifeboat men, coastguardmen, and few residents who are to be found in this lonely outpost.

HOW IT ORIGINATED

This is how the landship was evolved. During the war the Government laid down a light railway along the sands from Spurn to Kilnsea for the purpose of serving the Battery at Kilnsea, and particularly to convey heavy traffic. Since, the light engines had been removed and the line has fallen into disuse. One day recently, Mr Charles Hailes, (who was a lighthouse keeper at Spurn at the time) of Kilnsea, wanted to get from Spurn to Kilnsea in a hurry. An idea struck him. On the line was a small bogey, or truck: the propelling force was the problem. It was blowing hard at the time, and the thought occurred, "Why not fix a sail to the truck?" He consulted Mr Edwin Hodgson, another Kilnsea resident.

CINEMA SHEET AS SAIL

At the Y.M.C.A. there was a cast-out sheet used for a cinema screen when the Garrison Artillery men were stationed there. This sheet they nailed to a mast. They stepped aboard, a gale was blowing from the south, and almost before they had realized it they were off like a shot from a gun, at a mile a minute. The next thing was how to stop the "ship," as when they approached Kilnsea Battery they realized they were in for a smash unless they called a halt. Quick as thought Mr Hailes whipped out his knife and slashed the sail free, and even then the truck rushed along for a considerable distance under its own momentum.

IMPROVING THE "SHIP"

Since then the "land ship" has developed, a proper fishing vessel sail has been attached and suitable brakes attached. The trip from Spurn to Kilnsea has been done in three minutes, which represents a mile a minute. We were told that the "landship" can run to and fro manipulating the sails in all winds, excepting a dead north head wind, or a calm, which we have yet to experience at Spurn Head. A trip on the landship is an adventure to the stranger, but the residents are getting used to it now.

For a first hand account, we need look no further than pages 50 & 51 of Ronald Kendall's book 'Growing up on Spurn Head', which covers the 1920s and 1930s. Speaking of the sail bogie he writes:

'This was a unique contraption belonging to the Lifeboat Men to convey cans of fuel etc, for the Lifeboat and for transporting families to and from Kilnsea if the military vehicles were not available.

Two axles with flanged wheels were placed on the railway line, then a wooden platform with shaped pieces of wood at each corner for handles. A long plank about nine inches wide going down the centre and protruding to about four feet at either end, and four U shaped irons underneath was lifted up and placed with the irons fitting over the axles. There were two holes in the platform, one either end, for a mast (properly reinforced of course), which carried a lug sail. It was always a great thrill to ride the bogie. When there wasn't any wind we had to push it, get into a run and jump on, but when the wind was OK it could travel very quickly. Sometimes it would travel so fast the sail could be lowered quite a distance away from our destination. The brake was a shaped piece of wood that one held between the wheel and a reinforced piece of timber bolted into place on the underside of the platform. It needed a bit of strength to operate. Whenever the bogies were in use permission was needed from the WD. Therefore they were lifted off the line immediately after use.

I remember on one occasion a gang of us, without notifying anyone, lifted the bogie onto the line and began pushing it along, running and jumping on. As we came up to the bend near Chalk bank and going down a slight incline, we came face to face with Kenyon' (the steam locomotive). It was a case of all jumping off and collecting a few bruises as the bogie crashed into the train. The bogie was in a mess of course. We were reported to our fathers who read us the riot act, and so forth. Over the years there were quite a number of incidents with bogies, such as the one where a new man was conveying a couple to Spurn Point but lost control. He lowered the sail but hadn't the brake to hand. He told the couple to jump. The two men jumped but the lady was too frightened to move for a while but eventually she rolled off, cutting parts of her face etc.' On page 52, Mr Kendall also makes the only mention anywhere of a pump trolley being used on the Spurn Railway.

Jan Crowther's book 'The People along the Sand', adds the following details on the sail bogies on the line. On page 112, she records that a family called Fewster, who owned a bungalow near the lighthouse, were allowed to use the sail bogies when the railcars weren't running. Unofficial trips on the railway from Kilnsea by a Hull char-a-banc proprietor were advertised, but when the authorities found out, this practice was promptly stopped! (P116)

No mention of the sail bogies is made after the Second World War broke out, so one has to assume that their use ceased then. A military road was constructed during 1941 and 1942. The railway still continued in use, but was dismantled in the winter of 1951 / 1952.

A view of the railway mid 1920s, looking south from the top of the gun director tower on Godwin Battery at Kilnsea. The station was directly below. The road crosses from the beach to the Bluebell Inn off to the right.

A postcard of Spurn Head c1950. This is a view of the railway, looking south at the Narrows. The line was closed within 2 years of this photograph.

A sail bogie, army style c1925. Taken near the recreation room on Spurn.

A sail bogie, civilian style, on the Point probably mid 1920s. Notice the S shaped spoked wheels, very different to the ones on the army style bogie. The dog is helping!

A superb view of a sail bogie, probably near Kilnsea. There are 11 adults and 4 children on the craft! (image courtesy of Hull Daily Mail/MEN Media)

The sail bogie heading south down the Point. Photo probably taken the same day as page 81. (image courtesy of Hull Daily Mail/MEN Media)

Le curiosità dello sport.

Gli abitanti di Hull, in Inghilterra, servendosi di un lungo tratto di binario rimasto inoperoso dopo la guerra, hanno improvvisato un curioso tipo di "veliero terrestre", di cui già sono in uso parecchi esemplari che raggiungono notevoli velocità.

(Disegno di A. Beltrame).

Description for image on page 83

A fascinating illustration, taken from a newspaper published in Milan, Italy, from 1899 to 1989 and called 'Corriere della Sera'. On Sunday, 'La Domenica del Corriere' was issued free with this paper. Achille Beltrame (March 18th 1871 - February 19th 1945) illustrated the Sunday publication for nearly 50 years, and it is to him that this picture is credited. Note how closely the detail follows the photograph on page 82! The artist has used some license to add locals and their boats. The question is - how did journalists in Italy in the 1920s become aware of the Spurn Landship? A translation of the text beneath the wonderful image starts with the heading 'The curiosities of sport'. It then continues 'The inhabitants of Hull, in England, using a long section of track that was inactive after the war, improvised a curious type of sailing ship, of which several specimens are already in use which reach considerable speeds.'

Recreating a Spurn Legend

When, after renovation in March 2016, the Yorkshire Wildlife Trust opened the Spurn Lighthouse in Yorkshire, the idea of creating a replica 'sail bogie' or 'landship' was mooted.

The first item on our modern day agenda to recreate this historic vehicle was to locate suitable standard gauge wheels and axles, and so the 'Readers' Platform' in the June issue of the 'Railway Magazine' printed my request for them. Unfortunately, I received no suitable response from this, but a friend of mine on his travels had come across a suitable bogie at the former GNR station at Rippingale, South Lincolnshire, which is now a private residence. I contacted the then resident and owner of the bogie, John Scholes, and asked if it was for sale. He said yes, but there was a slight problem – there was a saddle tank belonging to a shunting loco named 'Dora' perched on it! I agreed to buy the bogie on the understanding that it would become available when the said tank was reunited with the loco, little knowing that the wait would be for two and a half years!

Having collected the bogie in November 2018, it was transported to a private residence in East Yorkshire and stored. The original landships were very basic and mostly wood, but ours would have a steel chassis, be more robust, and possess some rudimentary brake gear. The earliest bogies had no brakes, and were stopped by throwing a sleeper in front of the speeding vehicle! Unfortunately, not quite up to the standards of the present health and safety conscious age. Obviously, suitable wood is readily available, especially in Hull, which imports colossal quantities of it. Most of the woodworking was undertaken by my friend, Torkel Larsen, an expert with timber, and also incidentally the driving force behind the proposal to build a brand new pier at the nearby Yorkshire coastal resort of Withernsea. Rope and the fabric for the sails proved slightly trickier to obtain.

Ultimately, I sourced manila rope, (Ideally, I wanted hemp, but this was unavailable) 12mm for the rigging and 6mm for brailing the sail to the beams. Modern nylon and wire products would have been totally out of character. I then needed canvas for sails. Again, any modern fabric such as vinyl would have been inappropriate. A local maker of covers for HGV trailers had just a tiny amount of cotton canvas left from decades ago, and agreed to fabricate the sail out of two end pieces (hence the variation in colour in the finished product), just for the price of the labour.

The modern day mainsail is smaller than the ones used on the line in the 1920s and 1930s. This is because the Spurn railway had no obstacles or lineside equipment. No tunnels, nor overbridges at all. There is no usable track longer than sixteen metres left of the railway now, so our sail bogie could only ever be a static display if it were to stay at Spurn. Therefore, if it is to move under its own power (or rather using the force of the wind), our landship has to conform to the standard loading gauge. It is for this reason that our vehicle is square rigged like Viking longships, unlike the original bogies, which were gaff rigged. The compromise enables this bogie to be usable at any standard gauge preserved railway.

The Yorkshire Wildlife Trust kindly assisted us in delivering the landship to the longest section of remaining rail on the peninsula. The date was May 7th 2019, and despite a poor forecast, the day was breezy but pleasantly sunny. We had considerable difficulty clearing out the track so that the bogie could move at all, for the rails were extremely corroded. The conditions on the day demonstrated that the craft was clearly underpowered with the light coloured sail. Therefore, after the photoshoot, it was decided to order a larger sail, up to the very limit of the standard loading gauge for railways in Britain.

The new sail is over 62% larger and because we had used up the supply of original cream canvas we had to settle on a rather attractive shade of red – red sails in the sunset in fact! It has increased the effective sail area from 47.25 square feet to 77 square feet. Using Martin's formula for the weight of wind captured in a sail: $W = 0.004 \times V^2 \times A$ (where W is the weight, V is the wind speed in mph, and A is the area of sail in square feet), it has increased the force delivered by the wind from 4.725 lbs at 5 mph, to 7.7 lbs.

A wind speed of 10 mph now provides us with 30.8 lbs of wind in our sails. The figures for stronger winds do not bear thinking about!

On June 3rd, the landship was transported to the Derwent Valley Light Railway at Murton, York. Here we conducted braking trials, stability and drawbar pull tests, as well as having a very enjoyable day sailing the rails. We found that the bogie with no one on it required an 18 lb pull to overcome inertia, and the lower figure of 9 lbs when the vehicle was on the move. With two adults on board, the relevant figures became 22 lbs and 13 lbs respectively. The wind that day was about 15mph from the WSW, with gusts up to 30 mph and with the orientation of the DVLR being broadly west to east, we travelled from the western buffers towards the station. However, the line is rather sheltered and we frequently hit dead spots were the wind just died.

The next time that we took the landship out was on Sunday, September 15th. The Vintage Carriage Trust at Ingrow on the Keighley & Worth Valley Railway had kindly invited us to display the craft at their museum on their Heritage Day. Here, the sail bogie met up with 'Lord Mayor', one of the constructor's locomotives, built in 1893, that had actually helped build the Spurn Military Railway. A unique chance for two items of the railway's rolling stock to meet.

On Friday, November 8th, we had the opportunity of trying out the landship on the North Yorkshire Moors Railway at Levisham. The weather was atrocious, but more significantly for our bogie, there was little wind! However, we did manage to get a couple of short runs when the wind rose in the early afternoon.

I would like to thank the staff at the DVLR for their warm welcome and assistance on the day of the trial. Thanks are also extended to the Velocipede Society for information about the braking system we used, and Torkel Larsen, Rick Sharpe and Harvey Midwood for their input on the project.

The Spurn landship trials can be viewed on Youtube at:
https://youtu.be/oZ-rdVZHOzw

The bogie destined to be part of our Spurn Landship recreation. It is supporting a saddle tank from a steam engine at Rippingale, Lincolnshire, April 2017.

Torkel Larsen drilling the chassis at Welwick, East Yorkshire, in January 2019. The central boom is behind him and the passenger deck at the right of the image.

Torkel admiring the fruits of his labour on the lawn at Welwick in March 2019.

The earliest landships had no brakes. 2019 regulations suggest otherwise! Close up of the brake set-up. Note S-shaped spokes like the bogie on page 80.

Spurn Point May 2019, the photoshoot. I pose in my late father's captain's uniform, with the track at Middle Camp and the lighthouse in the background.

Spurn Point May 2019 again. A classic image with all the gang on the Spurn Landship. Is it the 1920s? Only the offshore wind turbines give it away!

Derwent Valley Railway, Murton, York, June 2019. The first real trial of the Spurn Landship. Torkel and Mary, my wife, do the honours.

Derwent Valley Railway, Murton, York again. Mary and I, with Rick Sharpe, who let us use his workshop to build the sail bogie. More wind needed!

The Vintage Carriage Trust, Ingrow, September 2019. The sail bogie meets 'Lord Mayor', one of the contractor's engines that helped build the Spurn Military Railway in 1915.

Ingrow again. Mary poses on the Spurn Landship as one of Keighley & Worth Valley Railway's diesel multiple units passes. Three types of rail transport in one shot!

Levisham on the North Yorkshire Moors Railway, November 2019. Becalmed at the signals, Mary and I await the next breeze!

Bibliography

Benfell, Roy – Spurn Lifeboat Station –The First Hundred Years, Privately published 1994 ISBN 9780952346708

Crowther, Jan – The People along the sand : The Spurn Peninsula & Kilnsea, A History, 1800 – 2000, Phillimore & Co Ltd, 2006 ISBN 9781860774195

Crowther, Jan – article 'The Ale-Houses of Spurn and Kilnsea'

Dobson, Edward – 'A guide and directory to Cleethorpes with an historical account of the place, to which is appended a perpetual tide table shewing the proper time for sea-bathing, according to the moon's age, 1850

Dowling, Alan – Historical notes on the leisure boat trade, plus the minutes of Cleethorpes Council meetings

Dowling, Alan – Cleethorpes : The Creation of a Seaside Resort, Phillimore 2005 ISBN 9781860773433

E.L.F. – Our Home in the Marsh Land, Griffith Farran Browne & Co, London 1877

Fellow of the Royal Historical Society - Holderness & The Holdernessians, London & Hull 1878

Frost, Howard – Sailing the Rails: A New History of Spurn and its Military Railway, Spurn Heritage Coast 2001 ISBN 095403080X

Greenwood, J – The Trent & Humber Picturesque Steam Companion, J Drury, Hull 1833

Heywood, Abel – A Guide to Cleethorpes & Grimsby, Glade Books 1909

Heywood, John – Illustrated Guide to Grimsby and Cleethorpes 1890

Jackson, E – Jackson's Guide to Grimsby Docks, Cleethorpes, and Neighbourhood c1890

Jarratt, George A – Memories of Spurn in the 1880s, Privately published 1990?

Kendall, Ronald – Growing up on Spurn Head, Privately published

Lloyd's Registers 1897 to 1927

Malkin, Larry, Stotham, Ann & Smith, Dorothy – This Peculiar and Remote Little School, The School at Spurn Point 1893 – 1946, Countryside Publications Ltd, Chorley ISBN 0861571649

Ward, R – Spurn Head Postal History, Yorkshire Postal History Society Publication No 22, 1988 ISBN 0907022138

Ward's Cleethorpes and District Illustrated Guide 1900